Scales Dog

ALEXANDER HUTCHISON was born and brought up in Buckie, a fishing town on the north-east coast of Scotland. He has worked on and off in universities, including 18 years in Canada and the USA, though he gave up being a literary academic some time ago. As a poet (and occasional translator) he writes in Scots and English. Currently he lives in Glasgow. Based on recent experience he has decided that while wishful thinking doesn't do it, a proper determination can make the cosmos perk up and take a bit of notice. "Mr Scales Walks His Dog," an underground perennial, was composed in the early seventies and drew praise from Lawrence Ferlinghetti and Michael Ondaatje.

Scales Dog

ALEXANDER HUTCHISON

CAMBRIDGE

PUBLISHED BY SALT PUBLISHING
14a High Street, Fulbourn, Cambridge CB21 5DH United Kingdom

© Alexander Hutchison, 2007, 2008

The right of Alexander Hutchison to be identified as the
author of this work has been asserted by him in accordance
with Section 77 of the Copyright, Designs and Patents Act 1988.

First published 2007

Printed and bound in the United Kingdom by Lightning Source

Typeset in Swift 9.5/13

ISBN 978 1 84471 330 1 hardback
ISBN 978 1 84471 541 1 paperback

Salt Publishing Ltd gratefully acknowledges
the financial assistance of Arts Council England

1 3 5 7 9 8 6 4 2

Contents

Deep-Tap Tree

'he is called the heron of oblivion'

To Freyja

I

Lady of linen cloth
blue flax flower

give me the girdle of a languid beast

II

Bone fitted   sinew fitted
tongue to tongue-tip

III

Fire-slit rider of the golden pool
and bristled field

here is my chastity sold to dwarfs
for a necklace of garnet

IV

Straddled-in-blood
keep me from the wounds of distance

Mr Scales Walks his Dog

The dog is so old dust flies out from its arse as it runs;
the dog is so old its tongue rattles in its mouth, its eyes were changed
in the 17th century, its legs are borrowed from a Louis Fourteen
bedside cabinet.
The dog is barking with an antique excitement.
Scales dog is so old its barks hang in the air like old socks,
like faded paper flowers.
It is so old it played the doorman of the Atlantic Hotel in *The Last Laugh*,
so old it played the washroom attendant too.
Scales dog is so old he never learned to grow old gracefully.
Scales dog bites in stages.
Scales dog smells of naphtha.
Scales dog misjudges steps and trips.
Scales dog begs for scraps, licks plates.
Scales dog is seven times older than you think:
so he runs elliptically; so he cannot see spiders; so he is often distracted;
so he loses peanuts dropped at his feet; so he has suddenly
become diabetic and drinks from puddles; so there is bad wind
in his system that came over with the *Mayflower*; so he rolls on his back
only once a week.
Scales dog is Gormenghast, is Nanny Slagg.
Scales dog is Horus, is Solomon Grundy.
His body makes disconnected music.
He is so old his eyes are glazed with blood;
so old wonders have ceased; so old all his diseases are benign; so old
he disappoints instantly; so old his aim is bad.
Scales dog is so old each day Scales urges him to die.
Scales dog puts on a show like a bad magician.
Scales dog squats as if he was signing the Declaration of Independence.
Scales dog is so old worms tired of him.
So old his fleas have won prizes for longevity.
So old his dreams are on microfilm in the Museum of Modern Art.
So old he looks accusingly.
So old he scratches for fun.

Scales dog was buried with the Pharaohs, with the Aztecs; draws social
security from fourteen countries; travels with his blanket; throws up
on the rug; has a galaxy named after him; Scales dog runs scared;
would have each day the same, the same;
twitches in his sleep;
wheezes.

Political Digression

I saw two go by
like dragonflies
    joined

a kind of
    intercourse
from tail
to thorax—

the dry whisk
of eight beating
wings

Climacteric

This time something threatens to give way entirely:
Ridgepole, roof-beam, whatever you imagine as lasting
This time will fail to remember words that fell so bright
And fast about we found no shelter but the storm itself.

Burning branches in stoves and stalls, juniper burning
And the place thick with the smell of it. Star-bane;
Lesion in the thew of space.

Even the confidence of God at knell of the hardest season
Withers and rots away.

These purposes splinter in a rented room;
Intention, surface, prospect before, behind
Is all some thriftless illusion
Drawn down in a trough of queer air.

I can guess at it—tailing, diminished,
Acknowledge a thread of worn profit,
Even an infection slowly taken—

Nature scourged by sequent effects:
No lamp of bronze, no drum
At the cross-tree—
                    Appetite
And intelligence and little else:
Blood loop on a dry beaten run.

Of Akbar

I render the catalogue
of Akbar: of Iskandar's horse
washed in the fountain of life;
of Amber Head, his tasselled bridle;
of courtiers astounded by the lingam of ice;

further of a bauble—a bound man thrown
to dogs; of enclave; of ambit; of mustering
fancy; as demons pound chick-peas for tiffin
along the torrent side.

I give you the red woman
spinning before her tent; leopard
and lion silent at the tomb
of Bahram Gur.

I would set this down by
close particulars: each hummock
and fold of land; of trees the tamarisk
and grey-skinned sycamore; of birds
assembled the ring-dove and egret
and crested finch.

Laila languishes
and the stream runs clear; the pricket
tumbles to scent-spattered ground.

The Dead-*Carn* Shifting Slowly in the Drift

Within limits of his competence which is love
Man makes a thing to demonstrate inheritance,
Assert the roots; draws stock from strength
As love draws breath from love's own kindling.

So in my mind-stem wakes this river
And mountains backing a coastal plain:
White Ash, the Bin, Ben Rinnes in calendar;
Wakes self, wakes county, established line,
Marked as the valid topography of mind
And changing matter, a judgement,
Whether larch-tassels crimson at shroving,
Whether dust at the door of an earth-house laid.
Wakes Badenoch the Wolf, skin webbed at his fingers;
Wakes fish from standing stones; wakes Culbin bells
Below marram and shore.

Flood cut open the bank;
Red clay and out-cropping sandstone
Curdled the silt-rust current,
Broke brimming in the firth
Like an opened vein.

Heraclitus pieced flow change and fire;
Heart and will at the river of desire.

A Slate Rubbed Smooth

Chronicle of the hunter of forms:
Of the white stag killed in the off-eye; grain struck
   dropped from the husk.
Given the distinction between what one does and what one is.
Between the world ignored and reckoned new;
Between perfect technique and perfect attunement;
Between this here now and everything else.

Willow and river-sand, rain-bangled water.
By Grantown fleet and Rothes to Fochabers' iron bridge,
And bothies tar-streaked by Tugnet at the mouth,
Sheer the Spey shifts.
Wind flattens grey-headed grasses,
Gulls lag or lapse to a sable sea.

Looking back to real beginnings, felicitous,
When the mind goes like a skipping stone across the water,
Planets at each dip, sun and simple air at every rise—
That man the master of hawks enjoyed his land free,
Had a hand-breadth of wax-candle to feed his birds
And light him to bed.

When he hunted, hawk and hunter shared the prey.

Riguarda

So let me set down
the wonder that begins
one glance from love
to love

how lightly we danced

a young girl gay
so grave and winsome

jeune pucelete
je sui sadete

joliete plaisans

learning to please
myself and my sister

so let me set out
one step from love

.

So let me set out
one step from love

not distant
not curious

in thrall
to that or this

but liable
ardent

intending

careless of graces
we labour to be clear
.

So let me set down
the wonder around
the one loving laughter

a smile so winning
on the fairest
face of calm

stone light ferry light
light off the water

at each place
my heart stops

to look at you
.

The Death of Odinn

Ominnis hegri heitir

The skerry stark, the sky
black-lead, the land's life
buckled hard in ice

nine days then hung
nine darks hung ganched
hung deadly down
the gallow's lord

horseman high in the thudding wind
the deep-tap tree a skittish ride

nine days nine darks
his own blind offering
wergild for the father fell

thirsting, fasting
hovering for wits of men
nine darks swept down
heart-stormed

howling at the root of light
rendering the deepest dark

more bitter than death
between his teeth
nine mighty songs
and the life to come

The skerry stark
the sky black-lead
landstream unfettered
weaving, sinuous

word flows on word like water
heart buoyant as a bird

and each thing done
built up from seed
          unfolds
to deep-tap tree.

The Moon Calf

'Tis happy therefore that nature breaks the force of all sceptical arguments in time.

— David Hume

Besides, error of judgement is not moral obliquity. Weakness of understanding is not depravity of heart.

— Radhakrishnan

The Moon Calf

Confute
confess

confound
confuttle

sell posters
for picnics

get fitted
with springs
.

Conjobbling
in the kitchen

or settling
down to conjobble
al fresco

cuts little
difference

either side
.

In a cosy
wee cubbyhole

malice
and avarice

clanging
like conkers
.

Ruminate
on that

she used
to say
.

Pressed
in a corner

they'll come up
with anything

beans dogs
knots in clothes
.

Remember
those spiders

that dropped
in the tropics?

mantids too
like birds

dissemble
.

Agrippa's hound
ran howling
away
.

No good
I guess

however you
arrange it

connexity
gone and no

contrivance
.

The bittern
booms

the bishop
plummets to
the floor
.

Beyond knowing
what it might be

nothing in practice

(foul smoke
up the flue
pipe)

some don't have
the courage

some don't have
the craft
.

The baker below
bereft of bread

the butcher

clean out
of bacon

.

The Usual Story

He was popular
she was generous

he had texture
she had grain

he fled
she followed

he cosseted
she stripped

he was silent
she was silent

she ate him up
he drank her in

she coughed him out
he rattled her taps

he tried flattery
she tried toadstools

he turned holy
she turned turtle

he changed utterly
she scarcely at all

she was Judith
he felt twinges

he was Bluebeard
she was not content

he became mystified
she became adamant

he found respite
she found out

he became a block of ice
she ran to seed

he became a block of stone
she started chipping

he dreamed his best dream
she sealed him in

Goosegogs and Gorcocks

Like that unprecedented day
the neighbour died, and I obliged
by carving the charm on a slip of cedar
tucking it under his tongue where he lay
linen-wrapped and bolstered in crimson
his necktie knotted the way he fancied.

Turning her brazen key
Frau Schadenfreude roused him early
cool, unruffled brought cornflakes and coffee
(his favourite start) with bacon ends
and soft boiled egg.

"What happened to the blood that tells?"
by sworn report our neighbour's first clear
utterance on waking.
He gave then some accounting
of penis bones in coons and weasels—warming
to the topic ("Not broccoli but baculi")
popping the cedar chip out like a tongue
to reinforce his point from time to time.

As butterflies pursued their usual
havoc on the lawn the company mocked
and mowed: "Does God forget?"
"Are nucleotides part of the binding to Prudence?"
Subtle as the sun at cloudless noon.

Within his linen shell our neighbour
disappeared by slow combustion.

We, of course, long since had tendered apologies
dropping out by the pantry window. Cake, beer
gammon and mustard we bore, and brandy and butter.

Knowing he had for these things no more use
no thirst to slake—no appetite to speak of —
once his fit was past and we were gone.

Surprise, Surprise

MacSween the corner butcher with confidence displays
for denizens of the city—'of toons the *a per se*'—
a vegetarian haggis, rank specimen of his craft.
Just what the creature might contain defeats surmise:
pinmeal and onions, nuts or beans, some dribs and drabs.
No gristle, no suet, no organ meats: no liver, no tripes
no lights, no heart. Instead of a sheep's paunch
potato skins with a saddle-stitch fly. Up the Mound
down Candlemakers Row the fix is in. The makars jump
the peddlers stump, the market splits wide open.

First *from a purely culinary point of view*—corned, curried
devilled, smoked and kosher haggis; haggis à la king; wee cocktail
haggis; haggis in a basket; haggis on the half-shell; *instant* haggis;
English haggis; haggis eclairs; Crimean campaign haggis, conceived
in Sebastopol, consumed in Balaclava; hot-cross haggis; haggis in
plum sauce; dessicated haggis; baked haggis alaska; chocolate mint-
chip haggis; non-stick convenient haggis; cucumber and haggis
sandwiches; junk haggis; whole-hog haggis.

Next *by haggis of a special bent*—weight-watcher haggis;
haggis for the moonstruck; haggis *nouveau*; haggis *grand cru*; 12 year
old vintage haggis matured in oak casks; 100 year old Kung Po haggis
drawn from the well without obstruction; "Bomber" Haggis; haggis for
lovers; lite, lo-tar, lo-nicotine haggis; Campdown haggis; drive-in
haggis; hand-raised, house-trained haggis, with pedigree attached;
haggis by special appointment; reconstituted haggis; nuclear-free
haggis; ancient Dynastic haggis sealed in canopic jars; haggis
quickstep; haggis high in fibre; haggis low in the opinion of several
discerning people; a haggis of the Queen's flight; Nepalese temple
haggis (rich, dark and mildew-free); hard-porn haggis; haggis
built to last.

Finally *objects tending to the metaphysical*—desolation
haggis; the canny man's haggis; haggis not so good or bad as
one imagines; haggis made much of caught young; unsung haggis;
haggis not of this fold; haggis dimm'd by superstition; perfectly
intuited haggis; haggis beyond the shadow of a doubt;
bantering haggis; haggis given up for Lent; haggis given up for
lost; haggis so good you think you died and went to heaven;
haggis supreme; haggis unchained.

Buchartie-Boo

Ponderous and pat
the poet rounds
things out: homely
as a kettle on the hob.

Far off, shore shingle
rasps: the cliff base
bare for shock.

By ingle-neuk
each word cut snug
sits plumb; slow breath
indrawn, the under-
croodle sounds like
roosting pigeons.

Hyne Awa: Nae Howtowdie

Hirplin hizzie
huddin roon

hurdies gaun lik
cogs in a clock

.

Balefire

hailsteens

hause-bane
trumpets

lava
bilin doon
the brae

.

Cack
an cabbrach

argie-bargie

yammerin onding
maistly blaa

.

Abeen
the grate

gash-gabbit Grieve

peymin here
dirlin there

.

Nae keek
nor sicht

a licht
redemptorie

aathin
lowpin ower
piky palin wire
.

For a lang
file noo—

comets
rockets

snotters
a snaa

blin lumps
a watter—

it's hardly
ivver been wither
t' ging oot
.

As birds
unmuffle

and braid
the air

Helix

for Sarah
far-faring

for her
attention

the bones
of a poem

and flesh
of circumstance
.

Something
quite dry

lean naked
insistent

cut to a T
for paltry
rhymesters
.

Back in
the days

when 'slate'
was bait

and 'slay'
was striking

spark
from flint
.

Take ear
to the wild boar's
tusky tantrums

snout
in a rush

the din
uproarious
.

Red rampage
means racket

contrivance
cacophany

bird song
dampened

three counties
round

when they
heard

the news
.

Nothing
at the start

with
the heart

unripe

the way
unhallow
.

Her face
was sallow

though
she smiled

and what
she spoke

came
simmering

through
the air
.

Stars
like dust

from a
pouncet-box

stars
like pins
.

The track
        the trail
the speckled
path

the hiss
of the print

of the sweet-
travelled path
.

The brake
itself:
        track
        tress
        tangles

its traces
untangled
.

The moment
in the dance

when the
dancers *move*

whisked round
in the counter

direction
.

By her
live words

and ghostly
words
.

By this
and that

by the
brain-ball

of your best
bosom friend

drawn out
and dried

for a
balsam
.

'By the
           clods
of our

horses' hooves
like ravens

flying

flecks
of foam
like snow

from my
bridle-bit'
.

By fifty
queans

that bared
their breasts

to him not
to ride on
.

By the
gullet

of the
swift dog
.

By the
lake that

seethed

when first
he stepped

in
.

As birds
unmuffle

and braid
the air

an instinct
like nitre

comes close
to confirm it
.

In pasture
lank foggage

though naked
not nigh
.

All days
and always

there are
times
to ignore

the advice
of friends

.

'Or-or
oh well

aurore
or else

so-so
hum-drum

sautez
sautez!

.

Barnache
(like
a barnacle)

tests the
briny sea

for sound

niddering
nattering

.

Perhaps
    you
can guess
who I am

perhaps
you can
say

yes that's
the one:

bedimmed
bedizened

befoulled
befuddled
.

Sad
master

of chop
and grind

cutting
slices off

other men's
songs
.

'Or-or
oh well

so-so
hum-drum'
.

The travellers
unwitting

forsake the
ravelled path

rasping
nattering

nottering
gassipping
.

'Powerful
witch

and a
silly one

working
her way

with those

not worth
her time'
.

Aurore
oh well

sorcellerie
.

He jumps
he jumps

his head

a slow
furnace
.

By rote
by roster

bedimmed
bedizened

a little

the worse
for wear

the travellers
open to wound
.

Les trops sincères
farcis faussés

mes bons confrères
rustauds roués

grinceurs
gnostiques

nigauds nacrés
ampoules faquins

les farfouillés

mes internés
mes tapotés
.

A rattle
of spoons

a niggling
of bones

a whistle
with all

tune gone
out of it
.

Foundered
dumfounded

by footpath
and grave-slot

the travellers
ravelled away
.

The motto:

slow
makes sure

the mode
liquescent

the emblem

the ciphering
snail
.

The coder
the counter

the maker
of monograms

trail-blazer

slow-rasping
slime finger

clue-worm
of the glistering
paths
.

All day
and any day

quivers

or quails
me rather

feathers
me away

disentangled

Nothing
at the start

with
the heart

unseasoned

nothing at
the close

with the heart
unreconciled
.

Word: speck
world: speckle

each fleck
each fair

contriving
a circle

where needfire
and sacrifice

go hand
in hand
.

Flyting

'for all this
and all that

and nature
sparking
at my elbow'

This is for emptiness
this is for gluttony

this is for mawkishness
thrashed to a foam

this is for blisters
on sisters in whirlwinds

for all those who need
to slide closer to home

This is slash-burning
to upstart opinion

each vice vouchsafed
each virtue sublime

invention exhausted
though scarcely invented

'the work of the self
in sufficiency of time'

This is for thin change
and careful advances

this is for fuckit
and do as you please

this is for fine words
that butter no parsnips

creeping to heaven
on well-padded knees

This is a labyrinth
hedged in with simony

nosing in circles
to subtle intent

this is for chalky thighs
speckled like sausages

grinding the teeth
of an old discontent

This is for namelessness
this is for avarice

this is for lunging
to deathless renown

this for necessity
razoring chances

howling and hounded
like bears around town

This gives the gist of it
this takes the sting from it

'one thing goes pulsing
then everything does'

this is specific
for whatever ails thee:

Go take up serpents
use beeswax and buzz

This is for *mousiké*
this is for *techné*

in fire-hail
and fire-flaught

the word has come down:
namelessness brainlessness
boasting an accolade

this is for trumpery
sparking a crown

This one will harrow them
garlic and bryony

Blocking and Grudging
and Pecking Apart

this is new testament
flinty then fluvial

saltires and salvoes
to uncluttered art.

Gravity One, Fielder Zero

I get here late
and what do I find?

That young Adolf's
pecker was chewed
by a goat; that
Gaspard's House of Perm
is not the coolest
place in town to call
from for a cab;
that some sort of
anaconda has taken
over the backyard.

Also the ghost of
Joe Sprinz still inhabits
Treasure Island — slack
jowled in amazement
craning up at the sky.

Teeth Lost When
Ball Hits Glove

Führer Cropped
By Billy On Rampage

Snake Digests
New Patio Furniture

Customer Dozes
As Hair Ignites.

"En Mai Quant Naist La Rosée"

In May
when the

dew sits
on the rose

and the ice
is drifted
away

the lad
that loves

is double
blessed

by joy
at night

and blithe
in the day

Oh God
Oh God

what will
my heart do

my love
just how
will it bear?

for she
that has

my heart
held
fast

is cruel-kind
as she is fair

from Famous Last Words

Lord Maunsie sniffed hard, and spit with satisfactory force toward a root at the side of the path through the park. The air was brisk; the sky above the Castle criss-crossed by vapour trails. It was not far through the Meadows to his chambers, and the old man relished the walk for the ventilation it offered his system, sweeping away the motes of musty jurisprudence. Suddenly he was brimful with an unexpected sense of well-being—he might even have called it happiness. It seemed so odd, so uncharacteristic of his ways and days, he smiled involuntarily and ducked his head. The feeling passed almost as soon as it had come, but when he reviewed the permanent—the habitual—blights that settled his disposition, and pinched down the corners of his judgement, he couldn't quite shake off the impression of sudden grace.

He sat down abruptly at the next park bench and removed his hat. His legs, the thighs particularly, felt the benefit of his exertion. Still, he was vaguely flustered. At a little distance to his left a grey squirrel busied itself on the ground underneath some elms, popping and rippling from one morsel to the next. Further off, against the back wall of the academy, some older boys were bullying a junior—rather half-heartedly, however—more it appeared as a matter of course: the enterprise lacking real vigour or viciousness. Maunsie, settled, felt no compulsion to intervene.

The young girl with auburn curls approaching with a friend was surprised but not alarmed when the old man rose quickly from his seat and came towards them. She said he didn't look scary at all; but she was embarrassed when he touched the hair at the side of her head and said what he did. No, she'd never seen him before she told the man who arrived with the ambulance, but he seemed to know *her*—he was smiling she said, just before he fell. "I thought they had chased all the red ones away"—that was what she thought it was he had said to her, and her friend said yes it was.

Within the courtyard of New College, on flagstones below the steps of the Hall of the General Assembly, and outside the offices of the Faculty of Divinity, twelve men are laid out in the pattern of a wheel. They are all dressed without ostentation in thick, navy-blue, woollen jerseys and grey-black trousers. Their feet are bare; their eyes are shut.

From a position alongside the eastern wall of the courtyard the statue of John Knox inclines its head to see what transpires just a matter of yards away. No other spectators appear to be present. Apart from the provocation of the number, and the rather banal disposition of the figures, nothing manifests itself as a clue to the event—if, in fact, an event it is designed to be.

On the stroke of one, as the signal gun thuds off from the Castle wall, one of the largest of the men opens his eyes and sticks out his tongue, with a motion that suggests the sudden opening of a drawer. Lodged, not stuck, but simply lying flat on the end is what looks to be a single, long, sharp, blue-pointed carpet tack.

Although this curious display could scarcely justify all the effort of directed attention, the statue of John Knox permits itself the sliver of a smile.

~

Well, we were sitting outside the Bistro, I think it was, eating almond cake with calvados, when this vision went by in red and blue, who might have churned the composure of anyone, never mind your excitable correspondent. But when I turned to point her out to H., he said in the blandest fashion imaginable, "O, yes, I've had her. Not bad. Had her several times as a matter of fact. That chap Benno I introduced you to last night, *he* had her for me; and Jack, nice boy, wonderful way with stone, penetrated her half a dozen times last year with wonderful satisfaction. In fact, I probably should ask him to try her one more time before he moves, or before I lose track of that notion altogether".

~

Ostler had been breathing the dank air of the cellar so long he had forgotten what drew him down there in the first place. His clothes had mildewed and rotted: some sacking in a corner was what he used now to keep out the chill. He ate nothing—there was nothing left to eat even if he discovered an appetite—but he drank some brackish water from one of the runnels, and that, apparently, was enough.

It was queer. He didn't feel ill. He didn't even feel anxious. Some kind of detachment or absorption (it was hard to tell which) had changed him, so that none of his previous attitudes of mind any longer had force. Stranger still, at the centre of this foul dark and damp, something resisted decay. Beneath all the remnants, strips and tatters, bits and pieces, something was clear and crisp and firm.

"Time to show a tip," thought Samuel Ostler, and in the darkest coiling fibre of that odd little man something shaped the desire for light.

Jessie found him—half in, half out of the crawl-space door. His face was white, his eyes were tightly shut. They had a difficult time lifting him clear. Once they had accomplished this, Letty, the gardener's daughter, caught at the hem of her father's coat and pointed. Her lips formed a perfect O.

Ostler's boots looked like sprouting potatoes. Pale-white and purplish hairy roots broke out of the leather uppers and rubber soles. Some had snapped off as they lifted him up. What had shocked the young girl, however, and what she pointed out now to the astonishment of her father, was a yellowish-white tip, just like that on a tulip or hyacinth, partly concealed by hair, but emerging untouched by rot, and tinged already with green.

~

"It's nae aw that difficult efter aw; the windae opens in: the catch at the back'll dae the trick. Ye hiv tae clim oot t' dae the tap—bit the ledge is plinty wide. Ye can grab the frame as ye work yer cloath."

Across the road, Miss King drew back her curtains to greet the day. The sight of the window cleaner perched on a ledge opposite gave her a start. She was not often nervous on her own account (though housebound she coped well enough), but she *was* apprehensive on behalf of others: her family, her grandchildren most frequently of course; but anyone crossing recklessly in traffic below, or lifting up from the airport nearby, might be touched, quite unconsciously by her concern, as Humphrey Duthie (or Humpty Dumpty as his workmates called him) was touched quite unconsciously now.

"Oh, I do hope he's got a good grip".

Police thought at first that Miss King had taken a fall. There was an odd twist to her arm, and the bruising around her neck was not so livid as to show up right away. One of the young detectives pounced on what they hoped would prove to be a principal clue. It was a rather grimy chamois cloth, lying just beyond her outstretched left hand. But it wasn't helpful after all. The window cleaner who had been on the street turned out to be working down to the far end at the estimated time of death. Several householders verified this. Duthie readily agreed the chammy could be his—he'd missed an old one earlier that week. No, he "hudnae droapt it"—he would remember that—"somebody must've nicked it".

Not much fell into place after that. Detective Sergeant Sparrow puzzled over the daughter's account that her mother had whispered, "Oh, do be careful"—or something like it—when she was first discovered; but it hardly seemed to matter at the time, and he wasn't sure it would help to crack the case now. If the Old Man eased up on the squeeze, things might get a bit clearer; but lately he'd been more menacing than helpful. "Somebody's going to have to take the drop for this, Sparrow," he said that morning, drawing his snot-rag slowly over his whiskers, "just make sure it isn't me or you".

∿

Next to City Chambers on the Royal Mile—just the flip of a stone as a matter of fact from St Giles Cathedral—the tawdriest kind of altercation is underway. Four drunks—two outright drunks, and two who might be at some other point in the day—are trading blows on the sidewalk, and spilling on to the cobblestones of the street. People watch in amusement or amazement. Passengers in cars stopped at the lights crane round to see.

The combatants move as if in slow motion. Many of the kicks or blows directed misconnect or fall on air, so the skirmish lasts much longer than it might. One of the abler bodies is armed with a metal walking support, half-way between a crutch and a staff, and with just the hint of a scythe in its shape and the manner it is wielded here, dealing cuffs to the head, buffets to the arms and shoulders—all laid on with bitter intensity. For some odd reason sound fails to carry, so we're spared the racket of cursing and vile recrimination. There is something medieval

and sordid and dreamlike about the whole affair: both ludicrous
and ghastly.

After a while, one of the total inebriates is draped over the edge
of the pavement; the other props against a wall. The abler bodies
break off, and seem prepared to leave. But a mumbled threat, the
wag of a finger, the merest sign of resistance or pugnacity in their
flapped-out opponents, and back they come with wrath rekindled:
a lurching kick here, another sideswipe clatter there.

No police appear; no one intervenes. Suddenly, as by a trick in
the air, the voices come through. "I never said that. I never. I'll
get ye. Christ, ye useless. I never."

Futile, repetitive, barbaric, we stand, we smile, we strike, we rise,
we stumble down once more.

～

It was simply the sound of his laughter I missed, among all the
other things I might have remembered: the riots, the palaces, the
empty carriages rolling up Highgate Hill.

Going to the Millbanks with that catalogue of horrors was perhaps
the strangest office of friendship; though B. claimed later I must
have failed to touch the deepest vein of morose delectation, since
the "unforgivable vice" went undiscovered—failed to be revealed
that is—it simply wasn't on the list the family maintained.

Then there were the bailiffs at Picadilly Terrace—confiscating
even the birds in their cages—and the flicker of mischief detected
in B. at his wedding: "With all my worldly goods I thee endow".

O, Annabella—cheerless Bell—and Caroline, mad, bad and dangerous herself, who when she asked, "Whose funeral is this?"— it came right past their estate—her husband made no answer.

Lord, all our scampering around! Italy, Greece, the Alps. That torrent in the Jungfrau, for instance—"neither mist nor water but a something between both," B. said—as if I *cared* by then, what with glaciers and avalanches, lightning, hail. B.'s cloak was staunch enough; mine no better than a cobweb. Then the next day it was his turn: bemired all over when his horse went up to its chin in that morass, after I had dismounted and got over well. Still, he took the joke well. That's the laugh that comes back to me now—as he spurred the horse to go on.

What else? Well, that day we sailed into Patras on the *Spider*. And the wild flowers we split when I left him on Kos. I kept mine till they crumbled.

Anyway. One other thing: in fact, it may be the chief point of interest. Fletcher told me—it was part of his "Correct accompt of every Perticler"—that at the very end, before he damned those medical assassins and turned to the wall, B. grasped his wrist and said, not in delirium but with some show of vehemence: "She hauled me by the hair of my head: how was I meant to say no?"

Could be Caroline—maybe Theresa—it certainly wasn't Bell. But I think it went back to the very first. No, not the cousin. The servant girl—whose name escapes me. *She* menaced him, he told me once. "A proper fizz he was in, Mr Hobhouse," Fletcher says— and that seems right. "How was I meant to say no?"

Switching Channels

I watch a mantid snare
a snack (returning to the self-same
spot) and realise that she could take
a score of snacks: snip-snap, snip-snap,
and scarce one second would elapse.

One flick over, a man
from Jodrell Bank displays
an image snared from radio waves
of spiral galaxies exploding (not
unlike our own perhaps though several
million times enlarged). We see the jet
of fire (or something like a fire) shoot
out one side (or something like a side)
and realise this cataclysm took two
lifetimes on its way. Not mine nor yours,
you understand: the Earth itself had
just as much time left again to spend
as has been spent on everything
that's been or here.

A quick review: I know
you know the speed of light: one-eighty-
six times ten times ten times ten miles
covered for one brief glimpse
of one iota.

So the yellowish smudge (quite
arbitrary yellow) against the blue (quite
arbitrary blue)—that spume of worlds
dissolving—had its birth times Earth
times two times speed of light
per *second* to get here (plus the time
it took to be compiled
on Channel Two).

Being plausible
about what might give mass
to this miasma the man from Jodrell
Bank jumps to pluck one word
("neutrino") from his hoard of words
and perkily confesses physics as we
know it now is dodo-like
to guarantee what's what.

So let me tell
you, so you know:

it is a mantis taking prey,
it is the disposition to believe,
it is a *bumbast circumstance*,
it is a beauty and a *bel esprit*.

At the *Brasserie Pique*

I spoke the language of my heart.
The pupils of her eyes dilated ever
so slightly. Dust motes danced
in the glow behind her head.

I questioned her in all official
languages of the region: Creole
Franglais, Urdu, Dutch. My every
imposition deftly turned aside.

Scarcely daring to lift my chin
and gaze, I offered up some guesses
at her name: Sabine, Angelika
Hilde, Anne. None seemed to fit.

There was not any word
would serve; nor any soaring
song which she could not
quite wordlessly surpass.

When I drew breath, she
took the last morsel of *crème
brulée*, rolling it slowly
backward over her tongue.

And as I shaped to speak
again, she neatly spat a pip
of pomegranate on the table-
top beside my hand.

The waiter a-hover by the service
hatch for nearly half-an-hour
sprang forward then, removed
some plates, withdrew the shaker

of salt, and with his *prix
fixe* smile upended our *Blanquette
de Limoux* in its bucket of ice
and bore them both away.

Fleurs-de-Lys

Sullen girls like lilies,
see them: sulkily listening
to music. Does duty put that
look upon them of languid
disinterest, lids downcast?
It may be duty (sitting where
they do), but beauty marks
them: pale and perfect, lily
flowers. Round and above them,
a cappella, voices winding.
Sullen, lovely, eyes averted,
devotees of a pure disdain.

Carbuncle's Thrashing of the Tub

Incontinent, furious,
flashing and groaning, a tide-race advancing,
long tangled in bum-gut, hard-bitten harbinger,
hemmed in by catamites, true king of the bakers of Turd,
habiliments quivering,
choking, sweeping, treading on everything,
left hand and right anointing the faithful—
'Bone-smoke and mustard'—
out spake the great Carbuncle,
and lo his railing words like a rancid
custard, green and grand, spread upon the land.

'O miserable, deep-down,
damnèd dependency (haddocks astounded,
bees' hackles wavering). Take this as given:
not one word that wakes. Not one sparrow
to warble five clear notes in a row.

Nothing but a mish-mash of morbid mud-babies,
all crust and no filling, doldrums and doggy-doo—
Jerkin and Larkin and farting around—an entourage
of entropic garglers: baffle-headed Matthew; Dew-drop
the doctor; Askr Dingwangle, rod bent hard over ice.

Nothing in the bowls but ghosts or cauliflower.
Nothing but dandelions lining your crop'.

(He paused to blow his husky flue;
intemperate, querning, thus renewed).

'Where are my *secret seeds* and *toylsom moles*,
my shakers and fasteners, limpid limpets,
leaven to drabness? Where are my horses
for slippery courses?

Nothing left here but finger-tickling and small
potatoes—the desolate Something (wrestler? rider?)—
Snuff and Dawdle at the Poodle-cutters' Convention—
Sammy Sowthistle meet Perigord Pie.

No lattice of chemistry; no subtleties of close
configurement. Nothing but a roll-call of customary
characters: Paul the Pine-bender, bending out anguish;
Tender Alice from Saskatoon.

Give me back my crafty bundles, moot-halls and hackbuts,
my *Regiments of the North Star*, my quadrants and compasses.

All vehemence gone—God's juice—to
a kind of confessional entomology: bugs in the pantry
and nothing upstairs. Alphonse Rutabaga, bilingual
as buggery; Gordie Dumpling, chokerman with heart'.

By hap and slip, mote clapped, moth clipped;
cupboards all cracked from stem to stern.

By tuffets of grass, by bushes and berries, in echo
of striding, by driveways, in road-paths, by stone walls
of gardens, out broke the great Carbuncle:

'Boil them like brisket; discard the broth'.

Inchcolm

This morning I saw
on the waters of the firth a diving
bird I never saw before, turning a nimble
loop to enter the wave, and the wonder
of green light filtering down.

What was it like
for the king—Alexander, when the boat
nearly foundered, and all might be tossed
in the swirl of the sea? Did he kick
his boots free? Did he call out by his
birth-right for men to assist him?
And how did they come to land?

None of these
things is reported with surety. But fear,
if he felt it, was followed by gratitude—
the gift of an abbey for the Inch of
St. Colum. "Lord, I was drowning. What
better can I build than this?"

Then chancel
and chapter-house rose on the island.
Stone flourished on stone. Upon the table
slab of the altar five wounds were cut
like stars.

"It is foolish
to shrink from what cannot be avoided."
This was the bread they broke to sustain
them. "Quicquid mali finxerit lingua"—
whatever evil the tongue composes
conscience may overcome.

What warmth
of the spirit must have wound itself
round them—only one social fireplace
beyond that in the kitchen—though something
burned in the wall of the Choir when
Richard the Bishop had his heart interred,
so his ardour became part of the fabric
of the building.

Today we have
come to the natural harbour on the lee
side of the isthmus, climbed iron rungs
to the pier-head, and followed a path
by the narrow neck of land to stand
in the grave-yard, the Relig Oran,
surveying what replaced Colum's
daub and wattle traces.

Kings of Scotland
and Norway, Danes that were slain
at the "bickering" of Kinghorn, all
have their rest here: some at a stiff
price, and some with due reverence.

It is still broad
day when I take the night stair from
the ruins of the Church, and climb with my
sleeping child in my arms to the Dormitory,
talking and singing, though she sleeps,
and sitting for a while in the recess
at one of the windows.

The last day of January,
and the weather being mild, the water will
offer no menace as we make our return, not even
when we pass by Aberdour, crossing the Deep of
that impious Mortimer, long consigned in his shroud
of lead, well short of the island for which
he possessed, by gift of his forebear,
the right of interment.

But now there burns
in my arms a burden lightly borne—her
hair like a cresset or candle in the dark,
her hair like a badge or blazon—my
darling girl.

Within this high-vaulted
chamber I show you to shadows: the dreaming
forms of those who sleep like mist, who looked
in their own way for what holds true beneath
the bewilderment of surfaces.

It was a cold uncertain,
isolate existence; lived besides in a tangle
of dogma, that wrapped in despite: rock,
grass, flesh, sea-thrift and sea-bird.

I hold you here
against distortion; knowing that love
is work, is hard we know as breaking stones,
and desperate distance even when
the breath comes close.

                    But patience
with yourself, patience with the love
of others is a law worth learning, a thread
of blood I give you as a bond; and the water
of the world to enter and feed there as in
your natural element, taking your place
and composure, folding life around you,
your father's breath like a tide
on the margin of sleep.

Carbon Atom

1

*..If tributes cannot
be implicit,
give me diatribes and the fragrance of iodine..*

— MARIANNE MOORE

An Ounce of Wit to a Pound of Clergy

Let's begin our panegyric: weft of wool
and warp of cotton. Tow a drogue at your stern
so you won't broach to. Abandon your tails
and cheek pouches. For loft, for distance
put the baffy back in your bag.

.

Who wants this mush of meat and fat: poets
of the pemmican (dried and pounded) school—
with bugger the berry to give it some taste?

Where it's grind me to powders, and cankering
creeds—with never a blink of primrose banks
never a hint of beech woods building.

.

Strip off your rags and bend the bow.
Get your ordinance full and flowing.

.

And scrape me rather some pepperpots of potency:
the grains of Paradise, the cubeb, the chili
the cayenne of Guinea, the pods of Sichuan.

.

Put worms to work, and moles to mark them.

.

I'd have us smile like a parcel of seraphs.
Not lolloping loose; not dying duckies.

.

Ladies in sable, come up, come in—
take the weight off your feet, take ease
of all your rasping parts.
.

Warty newts and fire-bellied toads
continue your aquatic and sociable ways.
Natterjacks of heathland and dunes (your loud
rolling call like a ratchet). Corncrake
of bogland and grasses; fugitive, invisible.
.

Aspect of all aslip and aslither: things
that tremble, things athwart. Come gastropods
come snails and limpets—sallow, blanch
and black-avisèd.   .
.

Things that scuttle, that squeal, or puff
themselves up, or launch themselves through
the air at intruders.
.

Take root all sprouts of *pseudoplatanus*.
Protophytes and protomorphs, let's get a move on.
With hooks and burrs and green helicopters.
.

Set with ardour bright and clear
beams, jambs, lintel and moulding:
an architrave of red-hot promise.
.

Eager and apt we bristle, we burgeon.

The hand of the glazier puts putty to the frame.
The pastry-cook pounds out his faintest concoction.
.

Knit up the bones of computation.

Let like kiss like.
Let bright affinity walk
in anklets of amber, in fillets
of silver.
.

Not ten go, but twenty posts out of your way.
.

Cool and open and tempting the vista.
The spiral of the condor vast and leisurely.
The bat at noon (anomalous) in twittering loops.
.

Let all things fused
transparent, opaque
enjoy diversity.

Snaps and scraps of quick allurement.

.

Stone-crop in succulent rosettes
of yellow-pink and crimson-green.

.

Penetration of the optic:
when all the down-draft of wintry webs
is wafted away.

.

O, the women in dove-grey
swimming suits!

the roundel windows
admitting the light of day.

West Coast Tally

"Cha'n uaisle duine na cheird"

Torridon: start with
rock split and the rowan
growing out of it—after all
that's right in front of my nose.

Lochinver: I thought he
was the Devil himself—clever
wicked, affectionate, haughty.

Bernera: not quizzical
insistent—with courage
and *largesse.*

Braes: words and wood.
*No man above his trade—*but
this one lofty, familiar: beyond
Cuillin ridge his line across the sky.

Alba

'Foedum' Tacitus said
the weather was. Well
better the weather foul
than the will
of the people.

Lady Scotter

Lady Scotter
had a daughter

used to swim
just like an otter

sleek and quick
along the river

so it made the
young men quiver.

Not the sort of
thing that Scotter

quite approved
of in a daughter.

Sparks in the Dark

Alice Pleasance Liddell
Interrupted some boys in mid-piddle.
"Desist, louts," said Alice,
"Or each tiny phallus
Will spark in the dark on my griddle."

Epitaph for a Butcher

Noo he's safely doon below,
They'll no mak puddens o Mr. Snow.
For loin o pork and gigot chop
The wifies cam in croods tae shop.
A always fancied (some fowk didnae)
Sweetbreads, ox-tongue, tripe and kidney.
Nane criticized his potted heid;
But *contra Mortem* nae remeid.

Jimp

Jimp she was:
neat as a needle;
sprightly, lively
slender as grass

Excuse Me for Saying So

But you look like Tuesday
was payday, and Monday had never
come. Like your backside has been slung
out the window for the last half hour.
Like you just met your wife and overtime
arm in arm. Like the car keys are in your golf
bag and the golf bag's in the river. Like your
plumber's helper just got pulled in by the police.

Aye, and you look like your nose was stripped
and varnished by mistake. Like crowdie was called
for, and mousetrap is all there is. Like someone
put the polish to your socks and not your shoes.
Like the cat crept under your duvet and farted.
Like somebody coughed in your soup.

Announcement

Ladies and gentlemen,
may I have your attention please?
This train is approaching Silence station.

Passengers may alight here for connections to Gasp,
Dither, Lilac, Bobbinquaw, Jawbone, Sundry, Zipper.
Passengers may also connect to Freshet, Raddle,
Bolus, Reptile, Grout.

Passengers may change for Lucrece, Posy, Quillet,
Yammer, Darkness, Greater Dark.
Also for Soth, Sarlic, Hope, Love, Treacle.
Also for Radisson, Palgrave, Salient, Fly-boy.

They may also change for Christabel and Falssemblant,
with a further connection to Daphnis and Chloe.

Passengers are requested to check items of luggage
and all personal belongings before leaving the train.
Passengers with guide dogs should note that the platform
will be available on the left-hand side.

This train will be arriving at Silence in a few
minutes' time.

Thank you.

By the Beef and Not Touching It

1

Crows on the roof

some starlings nesting
under the eaves—

gangway for racketeers
black and green and
glossy.

All of a dither
epiplectic as usual

not much to the ditty
whaup whaup.

.

Raucous and ready
with the slant remark

wide open by nature
to the cutting return.

2

Gauche, giddy, gruff
in a byway below

the confluence of folk—

like a basket of cats
at a festival bonfire

glowering and glozing.

.

From jangle and spit
to pork chops and
synagogues.

.

Cannonades
of amorous glances.

3

Old agony bags
the butcher's dog

is out for a stroll.

His eye would blench
the regard of eagles

his insides chirming
like finches in a pot.

4

Bring your backsides
to an anchor! — loud hail
from a foul corner—

sit down and give
us some news.

.

From croodling
and crinkling

slap-bang
into bafflement.

.

(A lovely fellow
really—

took his black drop
like a gentleman

half way between
the transit of Venus
and Mercury.)

5

I'm a pantologist
Lancelot says

I know everything.

My brother
was a pantomancer

she comes back:

couldn't for the life
worm his way into
socks.

.

Whaup whaup
wheedle deedle.

6

A pretty
cynomorphic
observation

on her part though
if you ask me.

Striking it off
like a damp match
on sandpaper.

Everybody gawping.

7

Took his black
drop (as mentioned)

just like a gentleman

hardly knew
what hit him

or how high up.
.

Some kind
of imaginary

disgruntlement
most likely.
.

The last thing
she growled:

Put that
serpent away.

Mind the Gap

Of course there is an error
in the cleanness of the sea, and
for the landing of eggs outside the
compound something must be done.
Whereas tea and honey are merely
in decline, the lemon slice has
taken a holiday and may not return.

The wind in the chestnut trees
I assume has been taken for granted.
Conversely, firing of the jackhammer
at 7.15 occupied my full attention.

It is not that the women are not
wonderful—they are—but that
they are out of the question.
Elźbieta in particular has
legs that go nowhere.

What is the matter with the
butter on that dish? Is it possible
I will forget the mixing of cement
that followed my early re-awakening?

Agnieszka could have been more
pleasant in a number of respects—
nevertheless, her lower lip has a
quality I do not discount: that is
as far as pinkness and durability
are concerned.

Can no one here fix a proper
time for appointments? The canal
is empty; the remaining ducks
are in a state of confusion.

As for myself, I would
take a tram. But number 6
runs away; whereas 13 and 12
come together, overcrowded with
unpleasant people. It is risible
what the taxi driver has suggested.

Well, nothing could be
further from the truth. I did try
the scrambling of egg; still the
marmalade was beyond my grasp.

What does Bożena think
she is up to? When she dances
it is plainly disconcerting.
Perhaps we should all sit down.

No, it is not my turn.
I think after all there was
something funny about that slice
of sausage. Whatever unravelling
you had in mind will probably
now have to be postponed.

Disappointment is everywhere;
but when notice is short, displays
of pique are not unforeseen. Adjik
has gone off at a tangent once more.
What happened to his finger is no
longer our concern. I suspect the
biscuits have gone off with him too.

Unfold the map, and re-affix
the dog. Perhaps the jam will work.
I did spot some pickles and preserves
in the cupboard in the bathroom.

Port side is always best.
On the green part there is nothing
that will serve. If it comes to that,
take care to salute the quarterdeck
when piped on board. All hands take
great offence if this be neglected.

Last Time

The last time I saw him
he was loath to take
his eyes off two frigorific
local fillies, pacing along
the Coogait—half way
between Bannister's bar
and the mortuary gate.

Council Debate Resumes

Like some beetle stranded
on its back, which with a
sudden twist, a jerk, flips
front and forwards on its
face again—elated, frisky
the provost picked up his
fankled thread once more

The Hat

I thought I saw you.
I thought I could see you
come in and wander round—
I thought I recognized the hat.

Wherever it is you've clambered
off to, is there anyone there
to twist a story, lift a dram?

I could have sworn it was you—
my hand is out—even now I'm
smiling, waiting to say hullo.

Citronella

Lemon
sponge she
used to make

with lemon
butter icing.

I could think
of worse things

than sinking
in again to that
light sponge
astringent icing

the length
of those cool
dark citrus
afternoons.

Sibilance: Swifts

Erratic, headlong
sibilant: swifts are hinges
creaking in the air.

Brief Praise Poem

for EM

Who dives deeper
into the darting
shoal of words,

and who draws
a sweeter draught
from Mungo's well?

No Point

1

Wouldn't wish to put
any strictures into this;
and even saying that—
it's done, it's there—
mention what you might
seek to avoid and you've
not avoided it.

2

Love or counterfeit wealth
haul in by all means if you
want it: desire, joy—felicity
without limit. That should do
for a start: since the thing,
however select or seductive it
may prove later, will certainly
take some time to get going.

3

Unbounded; untold.
Who would want to?—
no point in rushing
anything there.

Didn't Do

for Norman

Well, I'll tell you
what he didn't do:

he didn't have a neat
wee cunt and push it around;

he didn't lean on—or into—
not for a sense of *obligation*;

he didn't smear all over
like old tar on foreshore rocks;

he measured by what he admired
not by what he might get;

he thought there was more
to life than passable dentition;

he sometimes snarled and sometimes sneered
—but never at next door neighbours;

if he cosied up anywhere
he did it because he liked it;

he didn't say "ah hah hah" out
loud in buses just to draw attention;

he opted for chins and buttercups
rather than 'a forest of symbols';

his bucket always reached down
to the water in the well;

what it took he knew—
what it took to know he loved.

[98]

Annals of Enlightenment

Hume passes
into the absolute,
brace-girdled, without
concern.

James,
laird of Auchinleck,
as this transpires, lays
boisterous breath along
his doxy's shoulder,

elevates the skirt,
and takes her on the dust
of a stonemason's table,
some way below
the Castle hill.

.

In or out
of armour, which
would you rather—

cool release
of the *bon philosophe*
or Boswell's perturbation?

Much to be endured,
and little to be enjoyed?

or what mix in between?

.

At ten, a drum
for clart and creesh
on close and vennel.

The wind
in a shift lifts
leaves along old
Calton wall.

Pea and Ham

Like they were baith hunkert
in Hungrie Mary's kitchy,
someplace in Dundee—
suppin deid man's face soup
wi lang drappin jaas.

Unfinished Business

for CMG

The first door cracked back, and there they lay:
scummers of pots and flayers of horses; jaws that clamp,
words that stink; flowery potatoes boiled in their jackets;
dabblers in cytoplasm, dacoits and daddy-long-legs;
virtual realtors gazumping like crazy; rooks crok-crocking
from the tippy-tops of trees:

> Idle or daedal—
> which is it to be?

iron pumpers, counter jumpers, carpet fitters bristling
with a mouthful of tacks; tomcats, corncrakes, cute
bicuspids; all the little shining ones; all those that
would grudge you one jowl of the bell.

The second door swung, so more became clear:
tethered tups; tattered drapes; the slalom boys of Dandruff
Canyon; phagocytes, phylacteries, *polski ogorki*; the exhalation
of piled-up corpses; beaters of candy floss, fairground artists;
earnest persuaders with the integrity of tissue paper;
all those women who run as though their feet were on
strings instead of on legs; all those shrubs pruned
too soon and suffering die-back.

Shoulder to the third door, and as you would expect:
sweet saurian smilers; choppers and changers;
men in blue corduroy, ladies in jumpers; brandy bumpkins
buttered and bandy; r.p. flannel dunkers; polymathic magpies;
pertinacious prognosticators holding their noses; shit that sells,
bugs that burn; bellhops, cowflops, moderate restrainers;
tourists in chaps and spurs lining the fire break;
piners, whiners, dainty dinahs:

> (as gentle a set of worms
> as you are like to see)

here-I-come, hempseed, listless rival:
death's on the whistle like the wind through trees.

Round the corner and down the stairs:
polyglot cocksuckers; chirpy charmers; porkers and moochers:
bracken for breakfast, neighbours for lunch. Last but not
least: flies in putty; wise guys and warblers; sad wicks
in seas of wax.

Coda: Scrape it if you like into one big bag-pudding (plums,
suet, orange peel); simmer it slowly, and serve it in slices:
who's to say it won't last for years?

The Holt

for Ian

Sinuous
from shadow

unsheathed
and silver

no pounce-work
no grudge music

words are in
the breathing ground

this uncircum-
scribable air

Incantation

—beginning with a couplet from *Carmina Gadelica*
and with grace notes from the same source.

I have a charm for the bruising
a charm for the blackening
a charm for cheats and impostors.

I summon from the cold clear air
from the bare branches of the trees
from worms coiling under the ground—

charm against cruel intent
charm for neglect
charm against wicked indifference:

may it lie on the white backs of the breakers of the sea
may it lie on the furthest reaches of the wind.

A salve for those who would grudge against the poor
a salve for those who would harry the innocent
a salve for those who would murder children:

may it lie in the stoniest stretches of the hills
may it lie in the darkest shelving along the shore.

A salve for those that would cram
whatever life they have with possession—
for the rage of owning without entitlement
for the desperate murderous possession of things:

may it lie on the cloud-banks that range across the sky
may it lie on the face of Rannoch Moor in its remoteness.

A charm against mystification by doctors
a charm against deception by the self-appointed
a charm against horrific insistence:

from the breeze that stirs the last of the yellowing leaves
from the slanting of the sun as it falls through the window.

A salve against grasping
a salve against preaching
a salve against promises exacted by threat.

> Grace of form
> grace of voice
> grace of virtue
> grace of sea
> grace of land and air
> grace of music
> grace of dancing.

A salve against the uselessness of envy
a salve against denial of our own best nature
a salve against bitter enmity and silence.

> Grace of beauty
> grace of spirit
> grace of laughter
> grace of the fullness of life itself.

A salve to bind us
a salve to strengthen heart and happiness:

may it lie in the star-blanket there to spread over us
may it lie in the first light at the waking of day.

Carbon Atom

2

Oh yes! We cheered for more. But like a dancer
Now the doctor turned, with swift wide soubresauts
Bounded across the lawn, and disappeared indoors.

— CHRISTOPHER MIDDLETON

Scota and Gaethelos

Scota:

I'll start on the day when
we sailed away from the court
of my father. My husband the one
whose tongue unlocked the sense
of other voices. I must say he was
as much a wonder to me as I was
apparently to him. What he saw
then I don't recall; I just know
I wanted the same.

The sea is like mother-of-pearl.
The sky is pearl and blue and
silver. My face is turned to you
as the light wind shifts and lifts
the sail. We have all our best
people with us. Gaethelos, tell
me, what name shall we give
to this broad sea?

Send out your best constructed
thought to the star that takes us
home. You seem to me like a
green straight stem spilling light
into the air around you. There's
the tide. Have we all the casks
and gear on board? You be
the sheet and I'll be the tack.
The wind will hardly know
what to make of us.

Gaethelos:

Let me speak, for pity's sake.
I have a great burst of words
inside me. Nimrod's tower was
never as bad as this. What's going
on? I don't want the past pursuing
me. Sometimes my blood boils up
like a campfire pot. It's never
going to stop; and the only
thing that holds it back
is Scota's voice.

Sometimes I think she sees
another person altogether; like
I think she sees another person
now. The ship will do. I know
the blood that waits ahead.
Whether the boys will do is
another question. They'll have
to. I'll just keep sending them
back in until they do.

I was never one to say: wait
three days, deliberate; when you
get a bone sniff it first. I had
a dream last night of a bird
that gleamed above a mountain
I never knew. The air was damp:
not dry, no dust, no sand at all.

I cannot understand: she sees
me pure—aye, no, not chaste—
she sees the thing that drives
me, and she knows that I would
put a flame to anything at all.
She knows that. Love, stay that
side. I'll take the windward rope.
Tongue, temper, ever reined
in, couldn't say. Whatever we
do it'll have her name. Whatever
that green place I'll maybe
soar and see it too.

Coup de Foudre

There once were some people
who lived in a wood. And they
were shiny, shiny, shiny.
And the wood was special too.

Piece by piece they would
have the wood for themselves.
Only shiny ones could enter,
and shiny is for sure as shiny does.

One day each bole and crown
was ash—each branch and bud
(*tsk tsk*)—and all from a smidgen
of durable fire lobbed
in from the dusty beyond.

Heading in to the Bar

Strike a lout
and you'd better
strike home.

    Keep the moon
    from the dogs;
    keep the bairns
    off the biscuit

What a terrible
face to wear
for a wedding!

    (Don't show that
    tooth if you don't
    mean to bite.)

A stone on your
cairn—sharp Murdo
might add—

    *Clach air
    do chàrn.*

Or—as
my New Jersey
companion was given
to venture:

    *No suckers?
    No nuts?*

One Line at a Time

Because a harmony has no part in the inharmonical

    nor the swallow, nor yet the hoopoe

their several affections, active and passive, were all for the best

    whether essence of equality, beauty, or anything else

wrapped in a goatskin or some other disguise

    like the sound of the flute in the ears of the mystic

the terrible nature of her confinement

    although not the same as oddness

is not dissolved or decomposed at once.

(Selections from: *The Trial and Death of Socrates*)

KANTICLE

Since space is not a composite

    even poisons have their use

changing its meaning to suit our convenience

    resting reason on empty figments of the brain

the elimination of all personal freedom

    a world of the senses and a world of the understanding

would have to be an intuition

    sometimes covered with fruit sometimes with ice or snow

some transcendental ground of appearance

    the idea always true in itself.

(Selections from: *The Critique of Pure Reason*)

RHETORICAL DEVICES

Serious or trivial, just or unjust

    people must be kept on good terms

self-sufficiency is also a good—

    aptitude to learn, quick wits

the more so the more memorable

    games, relaxation and sleep.

Being able to be mocked, and mocking with grace

    they also nourish suspicions

if one thing is possible, then so is the other

    like dogs biting on stones

but not touching the one that throws them

    a kind of communal expediency

the same thing threatens them both.

(Selections from Aristotle: *The Art of Rhetoric*)

EPISTEMOLOGY

Kept on a short leash

 or smothered in many blankets

perception has this inexhaustible profundity

 a particular instance of rendering thanks

a pouring on of water.

How is it accomplished?

 assessment of plausibility

is as it is and not some other thing

 a stick to feel one's way in the dark

"one cannot speak of dogs without

 having a word for them"—

roots of this perversion go deep.

Yet all this is beside the point

 like brewing or pottery

stones fell because their end was downwards

 beyond expression of a sentimental attachment

a name, an image, a shadow

    the baby given to the breast

restlessness in sleep.

(Selections from *Meaning*: Polanyi and Prosch)

RECEIPT

It is an ideal occupation for children

    on a wet afternoon

put them head to tail in an oven proof dish

    and remove any pips

score as above or into little bars

    do not roll for this also toughens

cover with foil with a weight on top

    wrap the birds in the bacon rashers

melt the fat in a saucepan

    turn over when little bubbles appear

whip the egg whites very stiff

    then coat the other side

take out with a perforated spoon

    add watercress, fried oatmeal or skirlie

when cut it is a soft pink butter

    the gravy is served separately.

(Selections from *A Taste of Scotland*)

Mao and the Death of Birds

Because they took, he thought,
more than their fair share of grain,
Mao decided the birds must die.

It could be this embraced concern
for the common weal, but economics
has its own imperative.

How did they do this?

Well, all one day, as long as it took,
the people banged on pots and pans
—whatever withering cacophony
they could raise—to keep the birds
aloft. Denied a roost, they flew until
their wings could not support them.
The people gathered every one
and put the pots to other use.

Was this not fine? The people, thus
instructed, dined on all that died.
Mao might have smiled; and no doubt
gathered in his own fair share.

Next year, without the birds,
the insects all enjoyed a carnival
in turn. The harvest failed—
and failed again—until in millions
people died. Was this not then
resoundingly complete?

What Mao had to say when
all transpired, again, I must regret,
I have no note; but do recall
another claim he brought—with pride—
of intellectual numbers down: 'more
than any Emperor that came before'.

How that was done was less
spectacular than what removed our
feathered friends—merely
another bland imperative.

At least they didn't cook
them where they fell—he probably
would draw the line at that.

When arbitrary despots rule, we
all are thralled to blind obedience.
Innocent and ignorant the Chinese people
died; and songs and words of those they
killed will come again—though in
what form is hard to say.

But may some demon boil the bones
of Mao in Yangtse's seething flood
for evermore—with everlasting
death to his vainglory.

Cunty Fingers

I didn't say it in
the first place, though
I knew what was up:
butter and toast—fingers
of toast—no, I hadn't seen
it before, but I wasn't
sure if I liked it.

I didn't say anything
to her when it surfaced
again—and I couldn't say
if she smiled or not. She
cleared the plate, not me.

Hippertie-Skippertie

Hippertie-skippertie, heid lik a bee,
Bizzin roon fae flooer t' tree.
Kirr an kittle, come ower t' me,
Hippertie-skippertie, heid lik a bee.

Above Stromness

for GMB

Mist at midnight,
night-scented stock;

happily betrayed
in what we choose
to name or work:

in this case gilly-
flower cruciferous
in clove-scented air.

Yeeaiow

The cat comes in
disappointed that she
can't come in next door.

She strokes around and
exits. She's right of
course: it's getting in
where you want that
urges the purr
properly on its way.

True desire or true
necessity goes unsounded
here—though what
she wants is what
she gives voice to.

It's only fat-tail
off in a huff
to sit down outside
in the hall attempting
to disguise a further
disappointment in the
last little while.

Phytogeny

If I were a tree I'd be ancient:
girth increases; growth rings get narrower.
Canopy reduced as new wood steadily declines.
Then fungi come to hollow heart-wood;
lichen splash gardens on broken stumps beyond.
Retrenchment may go on and on
before sparse living crown declares decay.

Like a tree too I am become in this state
more attractive to other forms of life.
The fungi of course;
but *saproxylic* insects fancy me as well: sipping
or scuttling wherever they may.
Rare and uncommon beetles line up to take their turn.
In and around the root *mychorrhizae* engage themselves in ways
I'm not exactly anxious to enquire.
Mosses, ferns and *bryophytes* compete to keep me green.

"People are naturally drawn"—
it says right here—"to big old trees."
"Tenacious, timeless ..."
Phosphor at sunrise (Venus
the morning star)
silently combusts.

"Spirited though in decline" I'd say.
And best—as may hap—the whispering
below still clear
despite some flutterings above

Carbon Atom

"Now we are among the two innermost electrons of the carbon atom.
They mark out in their dance a neat sphere of electric charge. The four outer
electrons of carbon can come and go, whether in flame, in diamond,
or in DNA. But these inner electrons remain indifferent to ordinary experiences,
which cannot disturb their seclusion; they respond only to the nucleus within."

A lightning strike can knock us off our stride,
or radiation shifting in the sun's inside.

Make it ten to the power of three or four
and now you're talking: nerve enough to tap
"excuse me" on the perfect floor or plane
and swerve us into something special
not—*da capo*—same old stuff again.

We don't have much to do
with light that's visible: only
the rays that Roentgen
gazed straight through.

We never court seclusion.
What appears indifference may be misconstrued.
We do not sport the peacock flashiness of those lewd
variable neighbours in the outer port:
turning to fossil fuel or jewels or life.

Here in the inner ring just through the wall
our symmetry our charge our dance is all.
Nor strength nor love nor poison prove.
The core alone can stir us to remove.

No, No

Oh, no no no—
no—I wouldn't say
that—not hyenas.

No—no; well, not
exactly. I mean there
was the living body
they inherited—
there was that—
and what they later
got up to.

But—*no*—hyenas
is a bit strong—
wouldn't you say?
Just a touch.

Grass of Levity

Grass of levity
Span in brevity
Flower's felicity
Fire of misery
Wind's stability
Is mortality.

Simple utility
Fingered lubricity
Sprung from audacity
Known for rapacity
Any capacity
Is mortality.

Boundless servility
Neighbouring nillity
Primping polity
Bits of carnality
Vanity vanity
Is mortality.

What doesn't signify
Render or simplify
Impaled and crucified
Sat down or sanctified
Any identity
Is mortality.

Further and further space
Gruesome and human face
Graceless or born to grace
Here in this little space
Light in our little case
Is mortality.

[The first stanza is Anonymous and dates to 1609]

She Said

Your man fed
the birds in Ire-
land—or so
the story goes.

Finches, robins:
taught them to
come to his hand.

For all I know
he could have
led them in
snatches of song.

When he left,
the cat made
short work of

all their whistly
perplexities.

A Saturno Conditum

My friend, across the space
within this ancient hill-top town
everything gives breath to what
we wish or might aspire to.

Whatever the Volscians, whatever
those who built Cyclopic walls
before them felt, we feel.

Seeking beyond beauty or
ambition one at least to share
'an unguarded joke'
fireflies at night.

Hospes et humus—guests
a little while then gone.

.

Broom, elder, lemon-flower
the fragrance of valerian.

All this in a loom of light
is shuttled back and forth.
Swifts and martins carve the air.
Each olive tree on every
slope is shaped to give its
tiny blue-green song of praise.

Landing

The trouble
with heaven
is no passion

.

the trouble
with hell
is no love

.

In that case pure Purgatory
would seem to be
the best place to alight

.

trimming
the birches

skimming
the reed-beds

to splash-down

and shaking
the water from
our wings

Hole House Farm

The children
have got a bonfire going
in the back garden.

4 potatoes 3 eggs
and next to no idea
of how to go about it.

Three sheep
with long tails
in the middle distance
crunch their way
towards me.

Rain spots down;
the evening cools
to grey and green.
.

If I were to say
to you my heart is
like a log on fire

it wouldn't be true
not even close

but the nearest
thing I have to love is
this—is you—here
even when
the desperate animals

interrupt and some
dog makes the mistake
of barking all
strangers away.

Suona Per Te

The bell strikes five from the tower of San Michele:
the seventeenth hour has slid away; a late September sun
has spilled along and off the south-faced wall, and soon this
beautiful, ravenous, vast city in the valley of the Po, its elegance
and industry, its desperate imprecations, the crowds that bay
and sway in the catafalque of San Siro, for Baggio, Shevchenko,
Zanzara, Volpone; intricate pinnacles and ladders of sound,
confections, conspiracies; *minna di vergine* on the *pasticcio*'s glass
counter shelf, somewhere with saffron *risotto al salto*, somewhere
a slit or truncheon, sirens and mayhem; all subtle, immediate
human exchanges—*come va? come sta?* or *vaffanculo*—matrons
encrusted in coral and amber, and anywhere, everywhere grace
of flesh and eyes and favour, *ragazze* with backpacks or Vuitton
or nothing; in a morning (God, *less*—take two stops on the metro)
perfection in appearance: innocent and wary, or down the stairs
in boots and hair, *meretrix* incarnate, blatant tits and vacant stare
(not *this* one), which even the dim or insensate must savour;
in the heart of the city, Stazione Centrale; O Santa Sofia, I've seen
your handmaidens, have worshipped abashed and chap-fallen;
dritto, sinistra, tenere la destra—what turn shall I take now? My soul
in the Duomo's half-dark disconcerted, so I light a tall candle;
dove dovrei girare? alas the sad pigeons adrift in the piazza, alas for
the clapped-out green nag under Pepe Missori; O Lucifer, your
handiwork and artisans are legion, in CISCO and Squawk Box
and NYMEX, Komatsu; excepting, no question, the white flat-
topped sisters, or by Porta Romana in 'the street of the orchards'
Piera's *trattoria* (no nonsense, no menu, just stump up when she
asks you) — *carpaccio, tortino*, her *gnocchetti verdi*; O San Benedetto,
benedictions in return: each day, lips, tongue and throat slaked
by your watery benevolence; but all these, my brothers and sisters,
must founder: this night or next night we all will go under; if not
on the feast day of great San Michele, at four in the morning,
or in before lunchtime, or soon like the city in the hour that's
just struck now; shuttered or shadowless, in the flatlands
of Lombardy, Milano, unparalleled, lies down in the dark.

Acknowledgements

Thanks are due to the editors of the following, where some of these pieces appeared for the first time:

Agenda; *Ambit*; *Anthos* (Canada); *Ashen Meal* (USA); *Chelsea Hotel* (Germany); *DNA* (Canada); *Edinburgh Review*; *Ellipse* (Canada); *Fras*; *Lines Review*; *Lallans*; *Malahat Review* (Canada); *News and Weather* (Brick/Nairn, Canada); *Notus* (USA); *Painted, spoken*; *Poetry Scotland*; *Prism International* (Canada); *The Dark Horse* (Scotland/USA); *The Echo Room*; *Rubicon* (Canada); *Schema* (Italy); *Stand*; *Verse*; *Writing* (Canada).

Deep-Tap Tree. University of Massachusetts Press, Amherst, 1978

The Moon Calf. Galliard, Edinburgh, 1990

"An Ounce of Wit to a Pound of Clergy" was published as a pamphlet by Minimal Missive Maximum Missile Publications: Edinburgh, 1991.

"Incantation" was printed in *Carmichael's Book* (Artbook/Morningstar: Inverness/Edinburgh 1997).

"Epitaph for a Butcher" was the title poem of *Epitaph for a Butcher* (Akros: Kirkcaldy, 1997), which also included "Excuse Me for Saying So," "Lady Scotter," and "The Holt".

"Annals of Enlightenment" was printed in *Brilliant Cacophony* (The Scottish Sculpture Trust: Edinburgh, 1998).

"By the Beef and Not Touching It" was printed in *A Gathering for Gael Turnbull* (Vennel Press: Staines, 1998).

"Hole House Farm" was printed in *Love for Love* (pocketbooks: Edinburgh, 2000).

"Scota and Gaethelos" was printed in *Back to the Light* (Mariscat Press: Glasgow, 2001) with the following note:

> The legend of the founding of the Scottish people takes various meanders, some of which I've followed here, and some I've left alone. *Gaedal Glas*, they say, came from Greece to Egypt. His marriage to Scota, daughter of the Pharoah, is variously attributed to his daring and skill in arms, and to his skill in language. His comeliness is mentioned, as is his volatility. Before he died in what is now Galicia, he drove his sons to further exploration and settlement. In Walter Bower's medieval *Scotichronicon* there is an image of Scota standing serenely in the stern of their ship as it sets out on the original westward voyage. My poem, I hope, anticipates not only the shaping of a nation, but the great gathering of folk on both banks of the Clyde. Nimrod, king in Scythia, ordered the building of what was to be known as the Tower of Babel.

"Sparks in the Dark" was the title poem of *Sparks in the Dark* (Akros: Kirkcaldy, 2002), which also included "Above Stromness," "Alba," "*Coup de Foudre*," "Cunty Fingers," "Heading in to the Bar," "Hippertie-Skippertie," "Jimp," "Landing," "No, No," "She Said," "Sibilance: Swifts," "The Hat" and "West Coast Tally".

"*A Saturno Conditum*" was engraved in stone and mounted in the town of Arpino, Italy in 2002 as part of the international project *Il Libro di Pietra*. The full motto "*Arpinum a Saturno conditum*" is translated: "Arpino, founded by Saturn".

Carbon Atom selection first published by Link-light, Glasgow, 2006.

Copyright © Alexander Hutchison, 2007.